Don

by Iain Gray

Lang**Syne**
PUBLISHING
WRITING *to* REMEMBER

Lang**Syne**

PUBLISHING

WRITING *to* REMEMBER

79 Main Street, Newtongrange,
Midlothian EH22 4NA
Tel: 0131 344 0414   Fax: 0845 075 6085
E-mail: info@lang-syne.co.uk
www.langsyneshop.co.uk

Design by Dorothy Meikle
Printed by Ricoh Print Scotland
© Lang Syne Publishers Ltd 2015

All rights reserved. No part of this publication may be reproduced, stored
or introduced into a retrieval system, or transmitted in any form or by any
means (electronic, mechanical, photocopying, recording or otherwise) without
the prior written permission of Lang Syne Publishers Ltd.

ISBN 978-1-85217-419-4

Donaldson

MOTTO:
By sea, by land.

CREST:
An armoured hand holding a cross.

NAME variations include:
Donald
Donnald
Donnaldson
Doneld

*The spirit of the clan means
much to thousands of people*

Chapter one:

The origins of the clan system

by Rennie McOwan

The original Scottish clans of the Highlands and the great families of the Lowlands and Borders were gatherings of families, relatives, allies and neighbours for mutual protection against rivals or invaders.

Scotland experienced invasion from the Vikings, the Romans and English armies from the south. The Norman invasion of what is now England also had an influence on land-holding in Scotland. Some of these invaders stayed on and in time became 'Scottish'.

The word clan derives from the Gaelic language term 'clann', meaning children, and it was first used many centuries ago as communities were formed around tribal lands in glens and mountain fastnesses.

The format of clans changed over the centuries, but at its best the chief and his family held the land on behalf of all, like trustees, and the ordinary clansmen and women believed they had a blood relationship with the founder of their clan.

There were two way duties and obligations. An inadequate chief could be deposed and replaced by someone of greater ability.

Clan people had an immense pride in race. Their relationship with the chief was like adult children to a father and they had a real dignity.

The concept of clanship is very old and a more feudal notion of authority gradually crept in.

Pictland, for instance, was divided into seven principalities ruled by feudal leaders who were the strongest and most charismatic leaders of their particular groups.

By the sixth century the 'British' kingdoms of Strathclyde, Lothian and Celtic Dalriada (Argyll) had emerged and Scotland, as one nation, began to take shape in the time of King Kenneth MacAlpin.

Some chiefs claimed descent from ancient kings which may not have been accurate in every case.

By the twelfth and thirteenth centuries the clans and families were more strongly brought under the central control of Scottish monarchs.

Lands were awarded and administered more and more under royal favour, yet the power of the area clan chiefs was still very great.

The long wars to ensure Scotland's

independence against the expansionist ideas of English monarchs extended the influence of some clans and reduced the lands of others.

Those who supported Scotland's greatest king, Robert the Bruce, were awarded the territories of the families who had opposed his claim to the Scottish throne.

In the Scottish Borders country – the notorious Debatable Lands – the great families built up a ferocious reputation for providing warlike men accustomed to raiding into England and occasionally fighting one another.

Chiefs had the power to dispense justice and to confiscate lands and clan warfare produced a society where martial virtues – courage, hardiness, tenacity – were greatly admired.

Gradually the relationship between the clans and the Crown became strained as Scottish monarchs became more orientated to life in the Lowlands and, on occasion, towards England.

The Highland clans spoke a different language, Gaelic, whereas the language of Lowland Scotland and the court was Scots and in more modern times, English.

Highlanders dressed differently, had different

customs, and their wild mountain land sometimes seemed almost foreign to people living in the Lowlands.

It must be emphasised that Gaelic culture was very rich and story-telling, poetry, piping, the clarsach (harp) and other music all flourished and were greatly respected.

Highland culture was different from other parts of Scotland but it was not inferior or less sophisticated.

Central Government, whether in London or Edinburgh, sometimes saw the Gaelic clans as a challenge to their authority and some sent expeditions into the Highlands and west to crush the power of the Lords of the Isles.

Nevertheless, when the eighteenth century Jacobite Risings came along the cause of the Stuarts was mainly supported by Highland clans.

The word Jacobite comes from the Latin for James – Jacobus. The Jacobites wanted to restore the exiled Stuarts to the throne of Britain.

The monarchies of Scotland and England became one in 1603 when King James VI of Scotland (1st of England) gained the English throne after Queen Elizabeth died.

The Union of Parliaments of Scotland and England, the Treaty of Union, took place in 1707.

Some Highland clans, of course, and Lowland families opposed the Jacobites and supported the incoming Hanoverians.

After the Jacobite cause finally went down at Culloden in 1746 a kind of ethnic cleansing took place. The power of the chiefs was curtailed. Tartan and the pipes were banned in law.

Many emigrated, some because they wanted to, some because they were evicted by force. In addition, many Highlanders left for the cities of the south to seek work.

Many of the clan lands became home to sheep and deer shooting estates.

But the warlike traditions of the clans and the great Lowland and Border families lived on, with their descendants fighting bravely for freedom in two world wars.

Remember the men from whence you came, says the Gaelic proverb, and to that could be added the role of many heroic women.

The spirit of the clan, of having roots, whether Highland or Lowland, means much to thousands of people.

Chapter two:

Fields of conflict

**Derived from the popular forename of Donald, the
Donaldson surname, in common with the Gaelic
MacDonald, means 'son of Donald.'**

Ranked at 91st in the list of the 100 most
popular Scottish surnames, it is to be found all over
Scotland, although it first appeared in the extreme
southwest of the country, in Galloway.

In view of the fact that the Donaldsons,
in common with the Beatons, Connalls, Galbraiths,
Howisons, Kellys, MacCalls, MacGowans,
MacLavertys, Sorleys and several others are
considered a sept, or sub-branch, of the mighty Clan
Donald, or MacDonalds, this Galloway connection
should perhaps come as no surprise.

The MacDonalds themselves have strong
Irish roots, with Ireland a relatively short sea crossing
from the western seaboard of Scotland and with
Galloway the first area of landfall.

Bearers of the Donaldson name flourished
in the Lowlands of Scotland and the far-flung
territories of the MacDonalds that covered both

the Highlands and Islands and Inverness-shire.

As an important sept of Clan Donald – one of Scotland's largest clans and whose several branches include the MacDonalds of Sleat, Clanranald, Glengarry and Keppoch – the Donaldsons shared in both their fortunes and misfortunes.

This was to the extent that the early history of bearers of the Donaldson name, with the exception of those who lived in the Scottish Lowlands, is almost identical to that of those who bore the actual name MacDonald.

Of Norse-Gaelic roots, Clan Donald takes its name from Donald, 1st Lord of the Isles, a grandson of the twelfth century Somerled, known as the King of the Isles, and who was killed in battle at Renfrew in 1164.

Donald died in about 1250, and his descendants were stalwart in their support of Scotland's great warrior king, Robert the Bruce, with his descendant Angus Og and his kinsfolk such as the Donaldsons fighting at his side at the battle of Bannockburn.

This was in June of 1314, when a 20,000-strong English army under Edward II was defeated by a Scots army less than half this strength.

Ironically, it was a through a misguided sense of chivalry that the battle occurred in the first place.

By midsummer of 1313 the mighty fortress of Stirling Castle was occupied by an English garrison under the command of Sir Philip Mowbray.

Bruce's brother, Edward, agreed to a pledge by Mowbray that if the castle was not relieved by battle by midsummer of the following year, then he would surrender.

This made battle inevitable, and by June 23 of 1314 the two armies faced one another at Bannockburn, in sight of the castle.

It was on this day that Bruce slew the English knight Sir Henry de Bohun in single combat, but

the battle proper was not fought until the following day, shortly after the rise of the midsummer sun.

The English cavalry launched a desperate but futile charge on the densely packed ranks of Scottish spearmen known as schiltrons, and by the time the sun had sank slowly in the west the English army had been totally routed, with Edward himself only narrowly managing to make his escape from the carnage of the battlefield.

Scotland's independence had been secured, to the glory of Bruce and his loyal army and at terrible cost to the English.

As reward for Clan Donald's loyal support at Bannockburn Bruce proclaimed that, in future battles, they would be given the honoured position of fighting on the right wing of the Scots army.

Nearly 200 years later, in September of 1513, Clan Donald was led by Alexander MacDonald of Lochalsh at the disastrous battle of Flodden, where an estimated 10,000, Scots including James IV, an archbishop, two bishops, eleven earls, fifteen barons and 300 knights were killed.

The Scottish monarch had embarked on the venture after Queen Anne of France, under the terms of the Auld Alliance between Scotland and her nation, appealed to him to 'break a lance' on her behalf and act as her chosen knight.

Crossing the border into England at the head of a 25,000-strong army that included 7,500 clansmen and their kinsmen, James engaged a 20,000-strong force commanded by the Earl of Surrey.

Despite their numerical superiority and bravery, however, the Scots proved no match for the skilled English artillery and superior military tactics of Surrey.

MacDonald of Lochalsh was one of the very few Scots nobles to survive the battle.

The MacDonalds and their Donaldson kinsfolk also proved loyal to the cause of the Royal House of Stuart, supporting it throughout the abortive Jacobite Risings of 1715 and 1745.

In much later centuries and different arenas of conflict, Sir Frederick Donaldson, better known as Hay Donaldson, was the mechanical engineer to the British Army who was born in 1856.

A son of Sir Stuart Donaldson, 1st Premier of the Colony of New South Wales and who is referred to in *Chapter three* of this booklet, he became chief superintendent of Britain's Royal Ordnance factories.

Appointed chief adviser to the Ministry of Munitions on the outbreak of the First World War, he was selected to accompany Britain's Secretary of War, Lord Kitchener, on a special mission to Russia in 1916.

Their ship, *HMS Hampshire*, struck a German mine off the Orkney Islands while en route, and Donaldson, along with Kitchener and all but twelve others, was drowned.

One of his brothers, St Clair Donaldson, born in 1863 and who died in 1935, served from 1904 to 1921 as the first Anglican archbishop of Brisbane, Australia.

Born in 1884 in Haverstraw, New York, Michael Donaldson was a Second World War recipient of the Medal of Honor, the United States' highest award for bravery in the face of enemy action.

He had been a sergeant with the 165th Infantry Regiment, 42nd Division, when, in 1944 at Landres-et-St Georges, in France, with his platoon pinned down under enemy fire in a sunken road, he rescued wounded comrades who were lying out in the open; he died in 1970.

Also during the Second World War, Trose Donaldson, born in 1914 in Tacoma, Washington, was a recipient of the Navy Cross and the Distinguished Service Cross.

He had been a lieutenant in the U.S. Naval Reserve, serving near Cavite, in the Philippines,

aboard a repair vessel. In December of 1941
disregarding his own safety, he helped to evacuate
wounded and fight fires during Japanese air raids.

It was for these actions that he was awarded
the Navy Cross, while he was posthumously awarded
the Distinguished Service Cross after being killed
in action in April of the following year while in
command of a U.S. Army tug.

Taking to the skies, Air Commodore Edward
Donaldson, better known as Teddy Donaldson, was a
Second World War flying ace and the holder of a world
airspeed record.

Born in 1912 in what was then British
Malaya, he joined the RAF in 1931, and on the outbreak of war eight years later was placed in command
of No. 151 (F) Squadron, flying the Hawker Hurricane
fighter.

With eleven confirmed 'kills', including in
action during the evacuation of Dunkirk in 1940, he
was awarded the DSO and later transferred to air
gunnery school where he wrote an RAF training
manual, *Notes on Air Gunnery and Air Fighting*,
which was also later used by the United States Army
Air Force (USAAF).

Following the end of the conflict, in

September of 1946 he set a new world record for air speed flight of 615.78mph (991.00km/h) in a Gloster Meteor F.Mk4 jet aeroplane – a record that remained unbroken until 1953.

Following his retirement as an Air Commodore in 1961, he was air correspondent of the *Daily Telegraph* until 1979.

He died in 1992, and the aeroplane in which he set the world air speed record is now on proud display at the Military Aviation Museum in Tangmere.

In contemporary times, Mark Donaldson, born in 1979 in Waratah, New South Wales is a recipient of the Victoria Cross of Australia, awarded for gallantry and the highest award in the nation's honours system.

It was in September 2008, during Operation Slipper, part of the Australian contribution to the war in Afghanistan against the Taliban, that, in Oruzgan Province, as a trooper with the Australian Special Air Service, he exposed himself to enemy fire to protect wounded comrades and rescue an interpreter.

Chapter three:

Enterprise and philanthropy

One particularly noted bearer of the Donaldson name was the bookseller, printer and publisher Alexander Donaldson, who was born in Edinburgh in 1727.

Opening a bookshop in the Scottish capital in 1764, it was not long before he incurred the wrath of the London publishing and bookselling establishment by printing and selling cheap reprints of books whose copyright had expired.

The business thrived to such an extent that his older brother, John, expanded the venture by opening a bookshop in the Strand, in London, where the books printed and published by his brother in Edinburgh sold much more cheaply than those published south of the border.

This was a period known as the 'battle of the booksellers', and the matter was not resolved until the complex conventions governing copyright and reprint were eventually resolved by statute.

Despite frequent and costly legal actions brought against him, the canny bookseller made a fortune from the concern, as he also did from the twice-weekly *Edinburgh Advertiser* newspaper, which he had launched in 1764 along with John Reid.

A founding member of the Royal Society of Edinburgh, he retired from business in 1789 after purchasing Broughton Hall, a mile northeast of central Edinburgh, and it was here that he died in 1794.

Twenty years before his death, he had passed control of what had become the highly popular *Edinburgh Advertiser* to his son, James Donaldson, who was born in the capital in 1751.

A noted philanthropist, renowned for regularly doling out money to beggars, he died at Broughton Hall in 1830 – after having bequeathed £220,000 for the foundation of Donaldson's Hospital, for the education and maintenance of poor children.

One stipulation was that there should be a preference for children named Donaldson or Marshall – the latter having been his mother's maiden name.

Originally housed in what had been Donaldson's magnificent townhouse in Edinburgh's Princes Street, designed by the architect William Henry Playfair, the school also catered for children

who were deaf or suffered from severe language and
speech difficulties.

By 1938, by which time it had become known
as Donaldson's School, it catered exclusively for deaf
children, and in 2008 re-located to a purpose-built
campus in Linlithgow, where, as a National Grant
Aided School, it has facilities for 120 pupils.

In Scottish politics, Arthur Donaldson, born in
Dundee in 1901, was the politician who served as leader
of the Scottish National Party (SNP) from 1960 to 1969.

Working for a time as a journalist in his native
city, he left at the age of 21 with the aim of pursuing a
similar career in the United States.

But, once in America, he dropped his
journalistic ambitions in favour of a wholly different
career in the automotive industry in Detroit.

Although far from his native land, he
followed with interest the growing movement for an
independent Scotland and, accordingly, joined the
National Party of Scotland, forerunner of the SNP, as
an overseas member.

Returning to Scotland with his family in
1936, he settled to yet another career, this time in
farming, in Ayrshire.

It was here that in May of 1941, suspected of

subversive activities, his home was raided by police –
due to what was the support of some nationalists during
the Second World War for the Scottish Neutrality League.

He was arrested and interned for six weeks,
although never charged and no evidence of subversive activities was ever produced by the authorities;
he died in 1993.

In Australian politics, Sir Stuart Donaldson,
born in 1812 in London, settled in New South Wales
in 1844. Just four years later he was elected a member
of the first Legislative Council of New South Wales,
representing the county of Durham.

Elected in March of 1856 to the Legislative
Assembly of the first Parliament of New South Wales,
he later served for a brief period as 1st Premier of the
Colony of New South Wales.

Knighted in 1860, he died seven years later,
after having also served as a Commissioner for Railways
and as a member of the senate of Sydney University.

Back again to the original Donaldson homeland
of Scotland, Gordon Donaldson was the eminent historian who was born in Leith in 1913 and died in 1993.

Graduating from Edinburgh University with
an honours degree in history at the age of 22, he gained
a doctorate in the subject three years later from the

Institute of Historical Research, London, where he also won the prestigious David Berry Prize from the Royal Historical Society.

Following work as an archivist at the General Register Office for Scotland, he was appointed a lecturer in history at Edinburgh University in 1947, while from 1963 until his retirement in 1979 he was the university's professor of Scottish history and palaeography.

President for a time of the Scottish History Society and, following his retirement from Edinburgh University, Historiographer Royal for Scotland, he died in 1993.

His many books include the 1965 *Scotland: James V to James VII* and, from 1990, *The Faith of the Scots*.

Not only a noted historian and author but also a journalist, Archibald Donaldson was the Scots-Canadian who was born in Glasgow in 1926 and died in 2001.

Leaving school at the age of 16, he worked for the Ayrshire newspaper the *Ardrossan and Saltcoats Herald*, before serving with the Intelligence Corps during the Second World War.

Immigrating to Canada with his wife, Nina, in 1954, he worked for a time with the *Toronto Telegram*, later reporting from Washington as its correspondent from 1963 to 1966, before joining the Canadian Broadcasting Corporation (CBC).

As a CBC television producer, his many credits include the 1970 *The Military Man* and a documentary on Lenin.

A prolific author of historical works that include *Battle for a Continent*, he is best known for his popular biographies of Canadian Prime Ministers.

Also in Canadian journalism, Joan Donaldson, born in 1946 in Toronto, is renowned as having been the founding head of *CBC Newsworld*.

Joining CBC as an editor with *National Radio News* in 1967, she worked for a time as senior editor of *The World at Six*, and reported from Vietnam during that war – later producing a documentary film on the conflict based on Michael Maclear's acclaimed *Vietnam: The Ten Thousand Day War*.

Founding and heading *CBC Newsworld* in 1987, she suffered brain damage three years later after a road accident in Montreal.

In a coma for two years and left a quadriplegic, her career tragically came to an end.

She died in 2006, and Canada's annual Donaldson Scholarship is dedicated to her contribution to Canadian journalism.

Chapter four:

On the world stage

In other endeavours, one of the most prolific songwriters America has ever produced, Walter Donaldson was born in 1893 in Brooklyn, New York.

Responsible, in many cases along with lyricist Gus Kahn, for a string of enduring hit songs that include *Carolina in the Morning*, *Georgia*, *Makin' Whoopee* and *Yes Sir, That's My Baby*, he died in 1947.

Born in Edinburgh in the same year, **Pat Donaldson** is the internationally renowned Scottish bass guitarist who, in addition to playing in the early 1970s in the folk rock band Fotheringay, has recorded with the Canadian musicians Kate and Anna McGarrigle.

In jazz, **Lou Donaldson** is the American alto saxophonist who was born in 1926 in Bodin, North Carolina.

Over a career that has spanned several decades, he has recorded with fellow jazz luminaries who include Milt Jackson and Thelonius Monk, while he also performed for many years with the pianist Herman Foster.

Also in jazz, **Bobby Donaldson**, born in Boston in 1922 and who died in 1971, was the American drummer and session musician who played for artistes who include Count Basie, Helen Merrill and Benny Goodman.

In a much different musical genre, **Eric Donaldson**, born in 1947 in St Catherine, Jamaica, is the reggae singer and songwriter whose 1971 hit *Cherry oh Baby* has also been covered by a number of other bands who including the Rolling Stones and UB40.

Born in 1968 in Rockhampton, Queensland, **Helen Donaldson** is the Australian opera singer, trained at the Queensland Conservatorium of Music, Brisbane, best known for her roles in Gilbert and Sullivan operas that include *The Pirates of Penzance* and *HMS Pinafore*.

From music to the stage, **Norma Donaldson**, born in New York City in 1928, was the American singer and actress who, after a spell as a nightclub singer, toured with both Lena Horne and Harry Belafonte.

Acclaimed for her role as Miss Adelaide in the 1976 Broadway all-black revival of *Guys and Dolls*, she had been appearing in the popular U.S.

television soap *The Young and the Restless* when she died in 1994.

Behind the camera lens, **Roger Donaldson**, born in 1945 in Victoria, Australia, but later settling in New Zealand, is an acclaimed film producer, director and screenwriter.

A co-founder of the New Zealand Film Commission, films in which he has been involved include the 1977 *Sleeping Dogs*, the 1984 *The Bounty*, starring Mel Gibson, and, from 2008, *The Bank Job*.

He is also the father of the New Zealand sprinter **Chris Donaldson**, born in Auckland in 1975 and who, at the time of writing, holds his nation's record of 20.42 seconds over 200 metres.

From the athletics track to the snooker table, **Walter Donaldson** was the Scottish professional player who won the World Championship in both 1947 and 1950.

Following his retirement from the game, Donaldson is reputed to have broken up his personal snooker table and used the slate base to make crazy paving for his garden path; he died in 1973.

On the golf course, **Jamie Donaldson**, born in Pontypridd in 1975, is the Welsh golfer whose major championship wins, after turning professional in

2000, include the 2001 BMW Russian Open and the 2008 Mauritius Golf Open.

On the fields of European football, **Clayton Donaldson**, born in 1984 in Bradford, West Yorkshire is the English player who has played for teams that include Scottish Premier League club Hibernian and the English teams Crewe Alexandra and Hull City.

In American football, **Jeff Donaldson**, born in 1969 in Fort Collins, Colorado, is the former defensive back who played for teams that include, from 1984 to 1989, the Houston Oilers, and, from 1991 to 1993, the Atlanta Falcons.

In the rough and tumble of the game of rugby union, **Mark Donaldson**, born in 1955 in Palmerston, New Zealand, and nicknamed "The Bullet", is the former half-back who played for his national team, the All Blacks, between 1977 and 1981.

From sport to the creative world of art, **David Donaldson** was the noted Scottish artist who was born in 1916 in Chryston, Lanarkshire.

A student at Glasgow School of Art from 1932 to 1937 and later a member of its teaching staff, his many artistic accomplishments include creating a mural for the 1938 Empire Exhibition in Glasgow's Bellahouston Park.

A member of the Royal Scottish Academy and the Royal Society of Portrait painters, he was commissioned to paint the Queen in 1966, while eleven years later he was appointed to the prestigious post known as Painter and Limner to Her Majesty the Queen in Scotland.

Having painted many other prominent figures including the former British Prime Minister Margaret Thatcher, he died in 1996 – the year in which he was awarded the City of Glasgow Lord Provost's Award for the Visual Arts.

In the world of architecture, **Thomas Donaldson**, born in London in 1795 and who died in 1885, was the prominent nineteenth century English architect who, in addition to being the first professor of architecture at University College, London, was also instrumental in the foundation of the Royal Institute of British Architects.

Also in architecture, **John M. Donaldson** was the member of the American Institute of Architects and the National Sculpture Society who was born in Stirling, Scotland, in 1854.

Immigrating with his family to America at the age of two, as a young man he travelled to Europe to study architecture in Paris, Munich and Venice –

subsequently on his return to America becoming a leading light in the architectural renaissance of Detroit; he died in 1941.

While John Donaldson made a significant contribution to the architecture of Detroit in particular, **Jesse Donaldson**, born in 1885 in Shelbyville, Illinois, and who died in 1970, made a contribution to the United States in general.

This was through his radical overhaul and modernisation of the nation's postal service in his capacity from 1947 to 1953 as U.S. Postmaster General.

In the world of chess, **Elena Donaldson**, also known as Elena Donaldson-Akhmilovskaya, born in the former Soviet Union in 1957, is the Woman Grandmaster, indicating her rank as one of the world's greatest female chess players, who won the U.S. Women's Chess Championship in 1990 and 1994.

It was in 1988, while playing in an international competition in Greece, that she eloped with and later married the American chess team captain William Donaldson – the International Chess Master who was born in 1958 in Los Angeles.

Bearers of the Donaldson name have also excelled, and continue to excel, in the world of the written word.

Born in 1935, **William Donaldson** was the English satirist who gained fame under the pseudonym of Henry Root, authoring a series of best-selling books that include the 1980 *The Henry Root Letters* and the 1994 *Root About Britain*; he died in 2005.

Born in 1947 in Cleveland, Ohio, **Stephen Donaldson**, who also writes under the pen name of Reed Stephens, is the American mystery, science fiction and fantasy author best known for his *Thomas Covenant* fantasy and *Gap Cycle* science fiction series of novels.

His many awards include a 2000 World Fantasy Award.

In a different writing genre, **Julia Donaldson**, born in London in 1948, is the author best known for her *Gruffalo* series of children's books and other works that include the 2009 *Taby McTat*.

Born in 1907 as Frances Lonsdale, Frances Donaldson was the British writer and biographer who became better known in later life as **Baroness Donaldson of Kingsbridge**.

Her many works include the 1974 *Edward VIII*, the winner of a prestigious Wolfson History Prize and which formed the basis of the six-part British television series *Edward and Mrs Simpson*.

She died in 1994, four years before the death of her husband, John Stuart Donaldson, the British politician who was ennobled in 1967 as **Baron Donaldson of Kingsbridge**.

Born in the same year as his wife, he became a noted consumers' champion and, from 1976 until 1979, served as the Labour Government's Minister for the Arts.

In the judiciary, John Donaldson, ennobled as **Baron Donaldson of Lymington**, was the senior British judge, born in 1920, who served from 1982 to 1992 in the position of Master of the Rolls.

Elevated to the peerage sixteen years before his death in 2005, his wife was Dorothy Warwick, better known as **Baroness Donaldson of Lymington**, who served from 1983 to 1984 as London's first female Lord Mayor and from 1995 to 1999 as a member of the Press Complaints Commission.

She died, aged 82, in 2003.

In the field of medicine, **Sir Liam Donaldson**, born in 1949 in Middlesbrough, is the physician and surgeon who was appointed to the post of Chief Medical Officer for the United Kingdom in 2009, and who has also chaired the World Alliance for Patient Safety.

The Donaldson name is also to be found on the landscape – in the form of places and features that include the town of Donaldson in Marshall County, Indiana, and Donaldson Mountain, in Franklin County, New York.